2

3

Swirls Diaper Bag #2

Easy

designed by Lisa Gonzalez
Shown on page 4

FINISHED MEASUREMENTS

Approximately 8"/20.5cm tall (not including straps) x 13"/33cm wide x 4"/10cm deep

MATERIALS

Medium/Worsted Weight Yarn (MEDIUM 4)
Shown in:
Caron International's Simply Soft Brites (100% acrylic; 6 oz/170 g, 315 yd/288 m skein):
#9608 Blue Mint (MC), 3 skeins
#9607 Limelight (A), 1 skein
#9606 Lemonade (B), 1 skein

Crochet Hook, size US J/10 (6mm), or size to obtain gauge
Tapestry needle
Three large snaps

GAUGE: In single crochet, 14 sts and 13 1/2 rows = 4"/10cm, using a double strand. Gauge is not critical for this project.

STITCHES USED

Chain (ch) Reverse single crochet (reverse sc) Single crochet (sc)

PATTERN STITCH

Row 1: Sc in second ch from hook, * ch 1, skip next ch, sc in next ch; rep from * across, end sc in last ch, turn.
Row 2: Ch 1, * skip next sc, sc in next ch-1 space, ch 1; rep from * across, end sc in beginning ch, turn.
Repeat Row 2 for Pattern st.

NOTES

1. The Bag is worked with a double strand of yarn throughout to create a stiffer fabric.
2. A large rectangle is worked, then folded; gussets are attached to give the bag volume (see Diagram).
3. Pockets and Straps are crocheted separately and sewn on.
4. To create a more shaped bag, use foam board, plastic mesh, or other stiff material as an insert in the bottom of the Bag.

BAG

Using a double strand of MC, chain 76. Begin Pattern st, working in the following Stripe Sequence—75 sts, (counting ch-1 spaces), after Row 1.
Rows 1 – 13: MC; Rows 14 – 19: A; Rows 20 – 29: B;
Rows 30 – 35: A; Rows 36 – 48: MC.
Fasten off.

EMBROIDERED SWIRLS (see photo)

Before assembling Bag, embroider Swirls on RS (see #3 – Changing Table Blanket, for Diagrams and Embroidery Instructions for Swirls).
Place Swirls on one-half of the length of the piece, (the Back of the Bag), where they will not be covered by the Front pocket. Vary the direction of each Swirl, but keep about 14 rows between the outside edge of each finished Swirl and the beginning center of the next Swirl.

GUSSETS (make 2)

Using a double strand of MC, chain 16.

Begin Pattern st—15 sts, (counting ch-1 spaces), after Row 1.
Continue in Pattern st until piece measures 8" from beginning.
Fasten off.

SIDE POCKETS (make 2)
Using a double strand of MC, chain 12.
Begin Pattern st—11 sts, (counting ch-1 spaces), after Row 1.
Continue in Pattern st until piece measures 6" from beginning.
Fasten off.

FRONT POCKET
Using a double strand of A, chain 22.
Begin Pattern st; working in the following Stripe Sequence—21 sts, (counting ch-1 spaces), after Row 1.
Rows 1 – 6: A; Rows 7 – 16: B; Rows 17 – 22: A.
Fasten off.
Work another Swirl, larger if desired, on center of Pocket (see photo).

ASSEMBLY
Referring to Diagram, fold piece as shown.

Attach Gussets
Row 1: With wrong sides together, using hook and a double strand of yarn, join yarn with a slip st through both thicknesses (Gusset and upper corner of Rectangle); sc evenly down side to Fold line (bottom corner); work 3 sc in corner st; continue working across short edge (bottom of Bag) for 4" (to next Fold line and corner of Gusset), work 3 sc in corner; then continue to work up long edge of Gusset and other side of Bag to upper edge; do NOT turn.
Row 2: Working from left to right, work one row of reverse sc along all edges, working 2 sts in each corner.
Fasten off.
Attach remaining Gusset to the opposite side of Bag.

OVER-FLAP
With RS facing, using a double strand of MC, beginning at upper edge seam on one Gusset and working across the upper edge, join yarn with a sc; work 15 sts in Pattern st evenly across to the opposite side (seam). Work even in Pattern st until piece measures same as upper edge of Bag across to opposite Gusset. If desired, make the Over-flap longer, so that it may be tucked in when bag is full.
Fasten off.

SHOULDER STRAP
Using a double strand of MC, join yarn with sc to upper corner of Front (see photo); work across 7 sts (toward center of Bag) in Pattern st. Work even in Pattern st until Strap is desired length; join with sc at opposite corner on the Back.
Fasten off.

BLANKET STRAPS (make 2)
Using a double strand of MC, chain 6.
Begin Pattern st—5 sts, (counting ch-1 spaces), after Row 1.
Continue in Pattern st until piece measures 6" from beginning.
Fasten off.

Sew one end of each Strap to lower edge of Bag, 3" in from each side. Sew one-half of a snap to the opposite end of Strap, then sew the other half of the snap to Back of Bag.

EDGING

With RS facing, using a double strand of MC, beginning at upper corner where over Over-flap is attached to Bag, join yarn with a sc.

Row 1: Sc evenly across to corner of Over-flap; work 3 sc in corner st; work across short edge of Over-flap; 3 sc in corner st; work across long edge of Over-flap to opposite corner (where Over-flap joins Bag); then work across top of Bag to where strap joins Bag, work along edge of strap to opposite side where strap joins bag; do NOT turn.

Row 2: Working from right to left, work 1 row in reverse sc, working 2 sts in each corner, join with slip st to first reverse sc. Fasten off.

Repeat on opposite side of Bag, EXCEPT, because the Over-flap does not attach at the opposite end, work along the upper edge of Bag only, then along edge between Straps and along Strap edges.
Fasten off.

FINISHING

Using tapestry needle, weave in ends. Referring to photo, sew Side Pockets to Gussets, aligned with the bottom of the Bag; sew Front Pocket in place, matching Stripes.

Fold and roll matching Changing Table Blanket; attach to the Bag with Straps on Back of Bag when not in use.

Swirls Changing Table Blanket #3

Beginner

designed by Lisa Gonzalez
Shown on page 5

FINISHED MEASUREMENTS

Approximately 24"/61 cm x 18"/45.5 cm

MATERIALS

Medium/Worsted Weight Yarn (4 MEDIUM)
Shown in:
Caron International's Simply Soft Brites (100% acrylic; 6 oz/170 g, 315 yd/288 m)
#9608 Blue Mint (MC), 1 skein
#9607 Limelight (A), 1 skein
#9606 Lemonade (B), 1 skein

Crochet Hook, size US H/8 (5mm), orsize to obtain gauge.
Tapestry needle

GAUGE: In single crochet, 20 sts and 18 1/2 rows = 4"/10cm
Gauge is not critical for this project.

STITCHES USED

Chain (ch) Reverse single crochet (Reverse sc) Single crochet (sc)

PATTERN STITCH

Row 1: Sc in second ch from hook, * ch 1, skip next ch, sc in next ch; repeat from * across, end sc in last ch, turn.

Row 2: Ch 1, * skip next sc, sc in next ch-1 space, ch 1; repeat from * across, end sc in beginning ch, turn.

Repeat Row 2 for Pattern st.

NOTE: Blanket is worked lengthwise.

BLANKET

Using MC, chain 122 loosely.
Begin Pattern st, working in the following Stripe Sequence—121 sts, (counting ch-1 spaces), after Row 1.
Rows 1 – 15: MC; **Rows 16 – 25:** A;
Rows 26 – 40: B; **Rows 41 – 50:** A;
Rows 51 – 65: MC.
Fasten off.

EDGING

Round 1: With RS facing, join MC with a sc in any corner: * work 3 sc in corner st, sc evenly across to next corner; rep from * around, join with slip st to beginning sc; do NOT turn.

Round 2: Working from left to right, work reverse sc across to next corner, * work 2 sts in corner st, reverse sc across to next corner; rep from * around, join with slip st to beginning st.
Fasten off.

EMBROIDERED SWIRLS

(see Diagrams)
Using MC and tapestry needle, work Chain st as follows: Bring needle from WS to RS at A; form a short loop, insert needle into same place; keeping the loop under the needle, bring needle out at B; pull up loop against strand of yarn loosely. Repeat, working in a Swirl (see Diagram). Place 3 to 5 Swirls on the RS of the blanket (see photo), then work swirls on the WS of the blanket to make the Blanket reversible, if desired. Vary the direction of each swirl, but keep about 14 rows between the outside edge of each finished Swirl and the beginning center of the next Swirl. Weave in loose ends.

BAG ASSEMBLY DIAGRAM

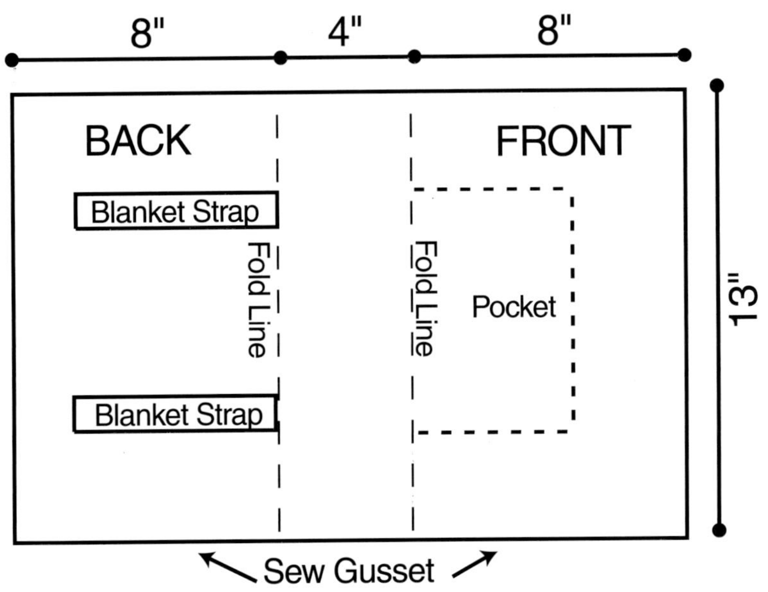

CHAIN STITCH DIAGRAM

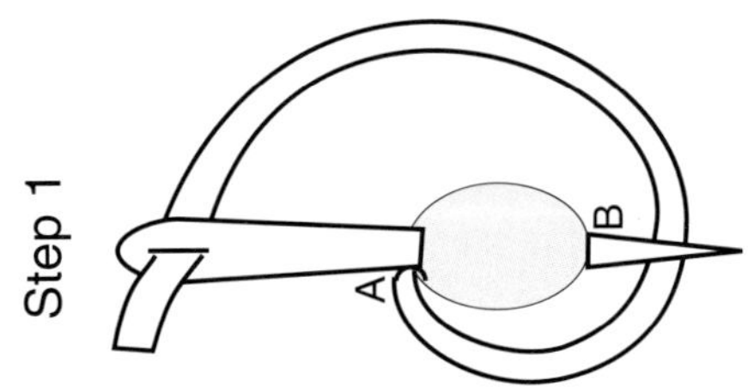

BASIC SWIRL

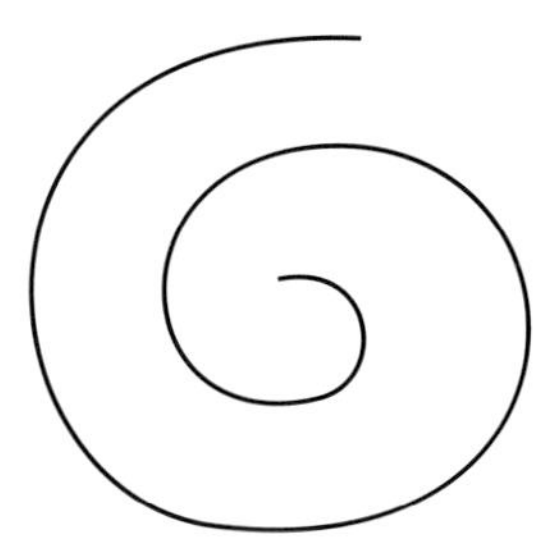

4

5

Octopus Rattle #4

Easy

designed by Deb Richey
Shown on page 9

MATERIALS
Medium/Worsted Weight Yarn (4 MEDIUM)
Approximately 1 oz each of two or more colors for Body and Legs
Shown in:
Caron International's Simply Soft Brites (100% acrylic; 6 oz/170 g, 315 yds/288 m skein):
#9606 Lemonade and #9605 Mango (MC)—use 1 strand of each held together throughout

Caron International's Simply Soft (100% acrylic; 6 oz/170 g, 315 yds/288 m skein):
#9727 Black (CC), small amount for eyes and mouth

Crochet Hook, size US H/8 (5mm)
Stitch marker
Tapestry needle
Small amount of polyester fiber fill or quilt batting
Small plastic egg, with a few beans or plastic pellets inside
Super Glue (to glue egg halves together)
Row counter (optional)

GAUGE: In single crochet, 18 sts and 24 rows = 4"/10 cm.
Gauge is not critical for this project.

ABBREVIATION
sc2tog: Single crochet 2 together – Insert hook in next stitch, yarn over and pull up a loop, (two loops on hook), insert hook in next stitch, yarn over and pull up a loop, yarn over and draw through all three loops on hook – 1 st decreased.

STITCHES USED
Chain (ch) Half double crochet (hdc)
Single Crochet (sc)

NOTES
1. Octopus Rattle is worked using 2 strands of yarn held together throughout.
2. The Head/Body is worked in-the-round, spiral fashion; do NOT join at the end of each round. Instead, place a marker at the beginning of the round and move it up each round to help keep track of the number of rounds worked.
3. This is the perfect project for using up small amounts of left-over yarn; mix and match from yarn stash for a unique, one-of-a-kind piece. Make a Rainbow Rattle, with each leg a different color!

HEAD/BODY
Beginning at the top of the head, using 2 strands of yarn held together in color(s) of choice, chain 2.
Round 1: Work 6 sc in the second ch from the hook; place a marker (pm) for beginning of round, and move marker up each round—6 sc.
Round 2: Work 2 sc (increase) in each st around—12 sc.
Round 3: Repeat Round 2—24 sc.
Round 4: * Sc in next 3 sc, work 2 sc in next sc; rep from * around—30 sc.
Round 5: Work even in sc (sc in each st around).

Round 6: * Sc in next 4 sc, work 2 sc in next sc; rep from * around—36 sc.
Rounds 7 – 12: Work even in sc.
Round 13: [Sc2tog (decrease) across next 2 sts] 18 times—18 sts remain.
Round 14: * Sc2tog, sc in next 7 sc; rep from * once—16 sc remain.
Note: Do NOT fasten off Body color(s). If working legs in same color(s) as Body, join new strands of yarn for the legs; Body will be completed after Legs are worked.

LEGS (make 8 around edge of Body)
Note: Working 3 hdc in each chain will cause the legs to curl naturally as shown in photo.

* Using 2 strands of yarn held together in color(s) of choice for leg, join yarn with a slip st in the back loop of any sc of Round 14; ch 24.
Work 3 hdc in second ch from the hook and in each ch to last ch, work 6 hdc in last ch, slip st in back loop of next sc.

If changing color(s) for next leg, fasten off.
Repeat from * for remaining legs, beginning each leg in back loop of next st after the slip st of the previous leg (there will be 1 slip st between each leg).

If working next leg in same color(s), do NOT fasten off.
Slip st in back loop of next st (st after the slip st of previous leg), ch 24; continue as for first leg.

After finishing 8 legs, join yarn with a slip st in first st.
Fasten off.

Stuff Body
Wrap the egg with a small amount of fiber fill, and insert into the Body, being sure egg is glued tightly together.

Decrease Round (s): Using Body color(s), working through both loops of sts, * sc in next st, sc2tog across next 2 sts; repeat from * around (in a spiral) until 6 sts remain.
Fasten off, leaving a 12" tail.
Using tapestry needle threaded with tail, weave through sts of last round; pull up tightly to close lower edge of piece; fasten off securely.
Weave in end.

EYES (make 2)
Using CC, chain 2.
Work 5 sc in the second ch from the hook, join with a slip st in first st.
Fasten off, leaving a 12" tail.
Using tapestry needle threaded with tail, attach eyes to upper area of Body (see photo).
Weave end into head.

MOUTH
Using tapestry needle and CC, embroider a smile under the eyes.
Weave end into head.

His and Hers Booties #5

Easy

designed by Deb Richey
Shown on page 9

One size: 0 – 3 months

FINISHED MEASUREMENTS
Length of sole: 3 1/2"/9cm
Width of foot: 2"/5cm

MATERIALS
Medium /Worsted Weight Yarn (4 MEDIUM)

HIS BOOTIES
Shown in:
Caron International's Simply Soft
(100% acrylic; 6 oz/170 g, 315 yds/288 m skein):
#9608 Blue Mint, 1 skein (MC)
#9607 Limelight, 1 skein (CC)

HER BOOTIES
Shown in:
Caron International's Simply Soft
(100% acrylic; 6 oz/170 g, 315 yds/288 m skein):
#9605 Mango (MC)
#9604 Watermelon (CC)

Crochet Hook, size H/8 (5 mm), or size to obtain gauge
Split-ring stitch markers
Yarn needle

GAUGE: In single crochet, 17 sts and 20 rows = 4"/10 cm

ABBREVIATION
sc2tog: Single crochet 2 together – Insert hook in next stitch, yarn over and pull up a loop, (two loops on hook), insert hook in next stitch, yarn over and pull up a loop, yarn over and draw through all three loops on hook – 1 st decreased.

STITCHES USED
Chain (ch) Double crochet (dc)
Half double crochet (hdc)
Single Crochet (sc) Treble Crochet (tr)

NOTE
Both styles are worked the same for Rounds 1 – 9.

BOOTIES (make 2)
Using MC, chain 9.
Round 1: Work 2 sc in second ch from hook, sc in next 6 ch, work 3 sc in last ch; working along opposite side of beginning ch, sc in next 6 ch, sc in last ch, join with slip st to beginning sc—18 sc.
Round 2: Ch 1, sc in first sc, work 2 sc in next sc, sc in next 6 sc, work 2 sc in next sc, sc in next (corner) sc, work 2 sc in next sc, sc in next 6 sc, work 2 sc in last sc, join with slip st to first sc—22 sc.
Round 3: Ch 1, sc in first sc, work 2 sc in each of next 2 sc, sc in next 6 sc, work 2 sc in each of next 2 sc, sc in next sc, work 2 sc in each of next 2 sc, sc in next 6 sc, work 2 sc in each of last 2 sc, join with slip st to first sc—30 sc.
Round 4: Ch 1, [sc in next sc, work 2 sc in next sc] 2 times, sc in next 8 sc, [work 2 sc in next sc, sc in next sc] 2 times, [work 2 sc in next sc, sc in next sc) 2 times, sc in next 7 sc, work 2 sc in next sc, sc in next sc, 2 sc in last sc, join with slip st to first

sc—38 sc.

Fasten off MC; join CC with a sc in back loop of first st.

Round 5: Working in back loops only, sc in each st around, join with slip st to first sc.

Rounds 6 – 8: Ch 1, sc in both loops of each st around, join with slip st to first sc.

Round 9: Ch 1, sc in next 15 sc, [sc2tog] 2 times, sc in next sc, [sc2tog] 2 times, sc in each of last 14 sc, join with slip st to first sc—34 sc remain.

HIS BOOTIES

Round 10: Ch 1, sc in next 13 sc, [sc2tog] 2 times, sc in next sc, [sc2tog] 2 times, sc in last 12 sc, join with slip st to first sc, ch 1—30 sc remain.

Round 11: Ch 1, sc in first sc, [sc2tog] 2 times, sc in next 6 sc, [sc2tog] 2 times, sc in next st, [sc2tog] 2 times; place a marker (pm) in first of the sc2tog just made ; sc in next 6 sc, [sc2tog] 2 times, join with slip st to first sc—22 sc remain.

Fasten off CC; join MC with a sc in marked st.

Row 12: Working in front loops only, sc in same st as joining, sc in each of next 19 sts, work 2 sc in next st, do NOT work last st (center Front of Bootie), turn; pm in second sc and next to last sc.

Rows 13 – 16: Ch 1, sc in both loops of each st, turn.

Fasten off MC.

Front Accent

Row 1: Using CC, join yarn with a slip st in free loop of first marked st, skip 1 st, work 6 dc in unworked st from Row 12, skip 1 st, join with slip st in second marked st.

Fasten off CC.

Row 2: Join MC with a sc in same st as slip st of previous row, work 2 sc in next 6 dc, sc in same st as slip st of previous row. Fasten off. Using tapestry needle, weave in all ends.

HER BOOTIES

Fasten off CC; join MC with a sc in first st.

Round 10: Sc in next 8 sts, hdc, dc, tr, tr, dc, hdc, sc2tog, sc, sc2tog, hdc, dc, tr; slip st between 2 tr on opposite side of bootie Front; tr in next st, pm on this st; dc, hdc, sc in next 8 sts, join with slip st in first st. Fasten off MC, leaving a tail approximately 10" long to work the last round, (tuck yarn inside Bootie while working next 2 rows); join CC with a sc in marked st.

Row 11: Working in back loops only, ch 3, slip st in sc, [slip in next st, skip 1, work 5 dc in next st, skip 1 st] 5 times, slip in next st, sc in next st, ch 3, slip in sc, turn.

Row 12: [Sc in next st, ch 3] 4 times, sc2tog across next 2 sc (do not work slip sts), [(ch 3, sc in next st) 3 times, ch 3, sc2tog across next 2 sc] 3 times, [ch 3, sc in next st] 3 times, ch 3, slip in last st. Fasten off CC.

Round 13: Pick up MC from Round 10; sc in both loops of skipped sts and free loops of worked sts, join with slip st in first st.

Fasten off. Using tapestry needle, weave in all ends.

6

Rainbow Pullover #6

Easy

designed by Lisa Gonzalez
Shown on page 14

SIZES: 3-6 (12, 18-24) months

CROCHETED MEASUREMENTS
Chest 17 (20, 21.5)"/43 (51, 54.5) cm
Length 7 (7 1/2, 8)"/18 (19, 20.5) cm

MATERIALS
Medium /Worsted Weight Yarn
Shown in:
Caron International's Simply Soft Brites (100% acrylic, 6 oz/170 g, 315 yds/288 m)
#9610 Grape (A), 1 skein
#9609 Berry Blue (B), 1 skein
#9608 Blue Mint (C), 1 skein
#9607 Limelight (D), 1 skein
#9606 Lemonade (E), 1 skein
#9605 Mango (F), 1 skein
#9604 Watermelon (G), 1 skein

Crochet Hook, size US K/10 1/2 (6.5 mm), or size to obtain gauge
Tapestry needle
Two small snaps

GAUGE: In Pebble st, 10 1/2 sts and 10 rows = 4"/10 cm, using a double strand of yarn

STITCHES USED
Chain (ch) Double crochet (dc)
Single crochet (sc)

Pebble Stitch
Row 1 (RS): Sc in second ch from hook, * dc in next ch, sc in next ch; rep from * across, end dc in last ch, turn.
Row 2: Ch 1, * sc in next dc, dc in next sc; rep from * across, turn.
Repeat Row 2 for Pebble st.

Color Sequence
Row 3 - Size Large only: Work 1 row using A/A.
Rows 3 (3, 4) – 16 (16, 17) - All sizes: Work 1 row A/B, 2 rows B/B, 1 row B/C, 2 rows C/C, 1 row C/D, 2 rows D/D, 1 row D/E, 2 rows E/E, 1 row E/F, 1 row F/F.
All Sizes: Work 1 row using F/G (F/F, F/F) – end size Small.
Sizes Medium and Large only: Work 1 row F/G – end size Medium.
Size Large only: Work 1 row F/G, 2 rows G/G – end size Large.

NOTES
1. Sweater is worked using 2 strands of yarn held together throughout.
2. Color changes are worked by changing only one strand at a time (see Color Sequence).

BACK and FRONT (both alike)
Using 2 strands of A (A/A), chain 23 (27, 29).
Row 1: Begin Pebble st—22 (26, 28) sts, turn.
Row 2: Using A/A, work Row 2 of Pebble st.
Begin Color Sequence; continuing in Pebble st, work even until 13 (15, 17) rows have been completed.

Shape Neck
First side
Row 14 (16, 18): Continuing in Color

Sequence and pattern, work 7 (9, 11) sts, turn.
Row 15 (17, 19): At neck edge, slip first st, work in pattern to end—6 (8, 10) sts remain, turn.
Row 16 (18, 20): Work across next 5 (7, 9) sts, leave last st unworked, turn.
Row 17 (19, 21): Slip first st, work in pattern to end—4 (6, 8) sts remain.
Fasten off.

Second Side
Row 14 (16, 18): Skip center 8 (8, 6) sts, join yarn with sc in next st; continuing in Color Sequence and pattern, work to end—7 (9, 11) sts, turn.
Row 15 (17, 19): Work across 6 (8, 10) sts, leave last st unworked at neck edge, turn.
Row 16 (18, 20): Slip first st, work in pattern to end—5 (7, 9) sts remain, turn.
Row 17 (19, 21): Work across 4 (6, 8) sts, leave last st unworked.
Fasten off.

Shoulder and Neck Edging
Row 1: With WS facing, join 2 strands of A with sc to shoulder at armhole edge; sc evenly across shoulder to beginning of neck shaping, work 2 sc in corner st, sc evenly around neck shaping to opposite shoulder, work 2 sc in corner st, sc evenly across shoulder to armhole edge, turn.
Row 2: Work Row 2 of Pebble st across shoulders and neck shaping
Fasten off.

SLEEVES (make 2)
Using 2 strands of A, loosely chain 13 (15, 19).
Row 1: Begin Pebble st—12 (14, 18) sts, turn.
Row 2: Using A/A, work Row 2 of Pebble st.
Begin Color Sequence; continuing in Pebble st, work even for 4 (4, 6) rows, turn.

Shape Sleeve
Increase Row: Inc 1 st at the beginning of next 2 rows as follows:
Ch 1, work 2 sc in first dc, work to end—14 (16, 20) sts.
Working inc sts in pattern, work even for 4 (4, 6) rows.
Repeat Increase Row—16 (18, 22) sts.
Work even until sleeve measures 6 (7, 8)" from the beginning.
Fasten off.

FINISHING
Overlap shoulders, Back over Front, approximately 1"; pin or tack together at armhole edge. Measure down 3 (3 1/2, 4)" from center of overlap on Back and Front; place markers for underarm. Sew Sleeves between markers. Sew side and Sleeve seams. Sew one snap on each side of neck. Using tapestry needle, weave in all ends.

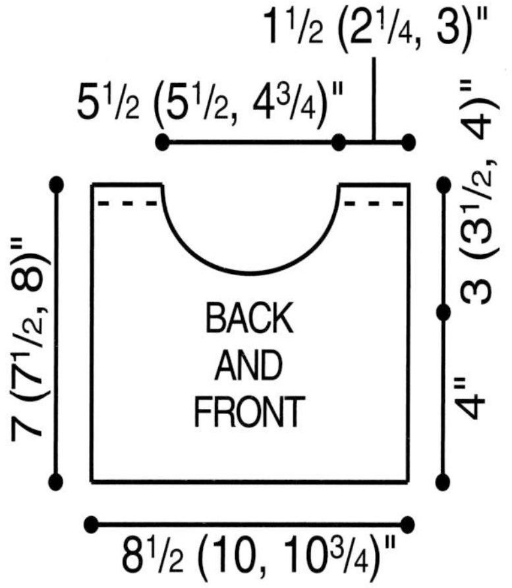

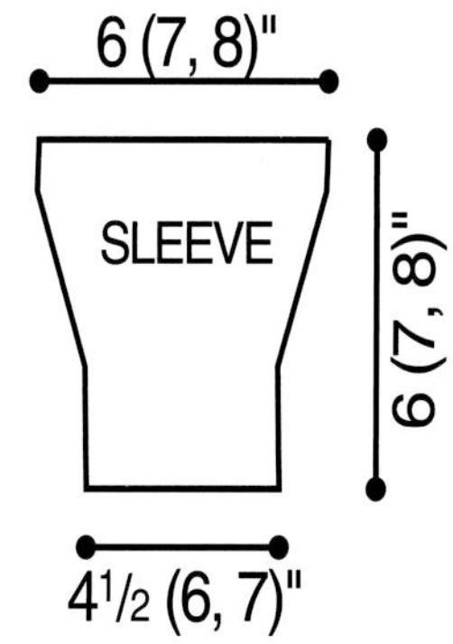

7

Baby Bugs and Happy Flowers Mobile #7

Intermediate

designed by Noreen Crone-Findlay
Shown on pages 17

FINISHED MEASUREMENTS
Hoop: 11 1/2"/29 cm in diameter
Flowers: 4 1/2"/11.5 cm in diameter
Butterfly: 3 1/2"/9 cm tall, wings 4 1/2"/ 11.5 cm from tip to tip
Bee: 3 1/2"/9 cm tall, wings 4"/10 cm from side to side
Caterpillar: 5"/12.5 cm long, body 1 1/2"/4 cm in diameter
Ladybug: 3"/7.5 cm long, body 2"/5 cm in diameter

MATERIALS
Medium /Worsted Weight Yarn (4 MEDIUM)
Shown in:
Caron International's Simply Soft Brites (100% acrylic; 6 oz/170 g, 315 yd/ 288 m skein):
#9607 Limelight (A), 1 skein
#9608 Blue Mint (B), 1 skein
#9604 Watermelon (C), 1 skein
#9605 Mango (D), 1 skein
#9606 Lemonade (E), 1 skein

Caron International's Simply Soft (100% acrylic; 6 oz/170 g, 315 yds/288 m skein):
#9723 Raspberry (F), 1 skein
#9727 Black (G), 1 skein
#9702 Off White (H), 1 skein

Crochet Hook, size G/6 (4 mm), or size to obtain gauge
Safety glasses
4 wire coat hangers
Needle nose pliers
Masking tape
Stitch marker
1 1/2" diameter plastic cabone ring
Yarn needle
Red crayon for cheeks
Polyester stuffing, approx 4 oz
Fabric glue

GAUGE: In single crochet, 20 sc and 16 rows = 4"/10 cm

ABBREVIATION
sc2tog: Single crochet 2 together – Insert hook in next stitch, yarn over and pull up a loop, (two loops on hook), insert hook in next stitch, yarn over and pull up a loop, yarn over and draw through all three loops on hook – 1 st decreased.

STITCHES USED
Chain (ch)   Double crochet (dc)
Half double crochet (hdc)
Single crochet (sc)   Treble crochet (tr)

NOTE
Always wear safety glasses when working with wire.

HOOP
Pull the coat hangers into a circle (ring). Using pliers, ease the bends out of hangers. Arrange the 4 hooks so that they are equally spaced, one in each quarter of the circle. Tape the 4 hangers together with masking tape.

Using pliers, bend the hooks up so they are slightly tilted in towards the center of the ring.

Wire Loops: Squeeze the hooks closed, and wrap the ends with tape to secure them.

Cover Wire: Using B, * join yarn with a slip st into one of the wire loops; work sc into the loop until it is well covered, join with a slip st to first st. Continuing to work sc over the wire, work around the upright stem, and then along the ring to the next upright stem.
Fasten off B.
Repeat from * around, covering loop, stem and ring in each section in the following color sequence: D, C and then E.

Tubes for Upright Stems (make 4 – 1 in each stem color):
Note: Place a marker (pm) at the beginning of the round, and move up each round, to help keep track of rounds.
Using appropriate color, chain 7, join with a slip st to form a ring.
Working in a spiral (do NOT join at end of rounds), work 11 rounds of 7 sc, join with a slip st to next st.
Fasten off. Pull Tube over stem.

Cabone Ring
Note: Work sc over yarn ends to cover them, working in the following color sequence: B, E, C and D.
Using B, join yarn with a slip st to Cabone ring.
Ch 1, work 10 sc over ring. * Fasten off. Join next color; work 10 sc over ring; repeat from * with remaining 2 colors, end join with a slip st to first st. Fasten off last color. Weave in ends.

Hanging Chains (make 2 – 1 using D and E; 1 using B and C)
* Using D, ch 50; join E, ch 50.
Fasten off. Matching Chain colors to Wire loop colors, pass Chain through Cabone ring, then each end through the matching Wire loop; fasten end securely around Wire loops. Weave ends into Chain.
Repeat from * for second Hanging chain using B and C.

HEAD
Face: Using E or D for Flowers, chain 3; join with a slip st to form ring.
Round 1: Work 6 sc in ring, join with slip st to first st.
Round 2: Ch 1, work 2 sc in each sc around, join with slip st to first ch— 12 sc.
Round 3: Repeat Round 2— 24 sc.
Round 4: Ch 1, work even (sc in each sc around), join with slip st to first ch.
Fasten off.

Embroider Face (see photo)
Nose: Thread a length of G in yarn needle, bring needle to RS of Face just below center and make a straight st; make a tiny st at the center to shape a curve.
Eyes: Make as for nose, slightly above and to each side of nose.
Smile: Bring the yarn to RS slightly to the side of one eye, and back to WS just to the side of the other eye; following curve, stitch the Smile in place with small sts.
Cheeks: Using red crayon, rub on Face for cheeks.
Eyebrows: Make one small stitch above

each eye.
Secure yarn by stitching in place several times on WS of Face. Trim ends.

Round 5: Flowers: Using A, ch 1, work even, join with a slip st to first ch—24 sc.
Round 5: Bugs (Antennae) Use A for Caterpillar; G for all others.
Note: Work first antennae above first eyebrow and second antennae above second eyebrow; this may mean adjusting placement of antennae in following instructions:
Ch 1, sc in next 10 sc; for Antennae [sc, ch 7, skip 4 ch, slip st in each of remaining 3 ch, and in same st], sc in next 2 sc; repeat [to] for second Antennae, sc in next 10 sc, join with slip st in first sc—24 sc.
Round 6 (All): Ch 1, sc in each sc around, join with a slip st to first ch—24 sc.
Round 7: Ch 1, [sc2tog] 12 times, join with slip st to first ch—12 sc remain.
Round 8: Ch 1, work even, join with slip st to first ch. Stuff lightly.
Round 9: Ch 1, [sc2tog] 6 times, join with slip st to first ch—6 sc remain.
Round 10: Ch 1, [sc2tog] 3 times, join with slip st to first ch—3 sc remain.
Fasten off, leaving a 6" tail. Using yarn needle threaded with tail, stitch opening closed.

FLOWERS (make 4)
Petals (make 5 for each Flower using C, D, E and B, using photo as a guide)
Leaving a 6" long tail; chain 6.
Row 1: Sc in second ch from hook and in each ch across, turn—5 sc.
Rows 2 – 4: Ch 2, work 2 hdc in first sc, hdc in each sc across, turn—8 hdc.
Row 5: Ch 2, work hdc in first hdc, hdc in next hdc, work [dc, tr, dc] in next hdc, hdc in next hdc, sc in next 2 hdc, hdc in next hdc, [dc, tr, dc] in next hdc, hdc in last hdc.
Fasten off, leaving a 6" tail. Using yarn needle threaded with tail, weave down to Row 1.
Using tails, stitch petals to center (Head) of Flower, overlapping them slightly.
Weave in ends.

BUTTERFLY
Using E and G, work Head.
Body: Using G, chain 3; join with slip st to form a ring.
Round 1: Work 6 sc in ring, join with slip st to first sc.
Rounds 2 and 3: Ch 1, work 2 sc in each sc, join with slip st to first ch—24 sc.
Rounds 4 – 6: Ch 1, work even, join with slip st to first ch.
Round 7: Ch 1, [sc2tog] 12 times, join with slip st to first ch—12 sc remain.
Round 8: Ch 1, work even, join with slip st to first ch.
Round 9: Ch 1, [sc2tog] 6 times, join with slip st to first ch—6 sc remain.
Round 10: Ch 1, work even.
Fasten off, leaving a 6" tail. Stuff Body; using yarn needle threaded with tail, stitch Body to Head.

Wings: (make 2)
Using B, work as for Flower Petal.
Join G to edge st of first row; work 1 sc in each st around the sides and top of the Upper Wings. Note: To ease around the curves, work 2 sc in the st that are at turning points on the Wing.

Fasten off, leaving a 6" tail. Using yarn needle threaded with tail, stitch Wings to Butterfly's Back. Weave in ends.

BEE

Using E and G, work Head.

Body: Using G, chain 3; join with slip st to form a ring.

Round 1: Work 6 sc in ring, join with slip st to first sc.

Rounds 2 and 3: Ch 1, work 2 sc in each sc around, join with slip st to first ch—24 sc.

Drop G; join E. Note: Nonworking yarn is left inside the Bee's Body.

Rounds 4 – 6: Ch 1, work even, join with slip st to first ch.

Drop E, pick up G.

Round 7: Ch 1, [sc2tog] 12 times, join with slip st to first ch—12 sc remain.

Round 8: Ch 1, work even, join with slip st to first ch.

Drop G, pick up E.

Round 9: Ch 1, [sc2tog] 6 times, join with slip st to first ch—6 sc remain.

Round 10: Ch 1, work even.

Fasten off, leaving a 6" tail. Stuff Body; using yarn needle threaded with tail, stitch Body to Head.

Wings (make 2)

Using H, chain 6; join with slip st to form a ring.

Round 1: Work 6 sc in ring, join with slip st to first sc.

Rounds 2 and 3: Ch 1, work 2 sc in each sc around, join with slip st to first ch—24 sc.

Round 4: Ch 1, work even, join with slip st to first ch.

Fasten off, leaving a 6" tail. Using yarn needle threaded with tail, stitch Wings to Body.

CATERPILLAR

Using E and A, work Head.

Body – First Section: Using A, ch 3; join with slip st to form a ring.

Round 1: Work 6 sc in ring, join with slip st to first sc.

Rounds 2 and 3: Ch 1, work 2 sc in each sc around, join with slip st to first ch—24 sc.

Rounds 4 – 6: Ch 1, work even, join with slip st to first ch.

Round 7: Ch 1, [sc2tog] 12 times, join with slip st to first ch—12 sc remain.

Round 8: Ch 1, work even, join with slip st to first ch.

Round 9: Ch 1, [sc2tog] 6 times, join with slip st to first ch—6 sc remain.

Round 10: Ch 1, work even.

Do NOT fasten off; stuff First Section.

Body – Second Section: Continuing with A, work Rounds 1 – 10 as for First Section.

Fasten off, leaving a 6" tail. Stuff Second Section; using yarn needle threaded with tail, stitch Body to Head.

LADYBUG

Using E and G, work Head.

Body: Using G, ch 3; join with slip st to form a ring.

Round 1: Work 6 sc in ring, join with slip st to first sc.

Rounds 2 and 3: Ch 1, work 2 sc in each sc around, join with slip st to first ch—24 sc.

Fasten off G, join F.

Rounds 4 – 6: Ch 1, work even, join with slip st to first ch.

Round 7: Ch 1, [sc2tog] 12 times, join with slip st to first ch—12 sc remain.

Round 8: Ch 1, work even, join with slip st to first ch.
Round 9: Ch 1, [sc2tog] 6 times, join with slip st to first ch—6 sc remain.
Stuff Body.
Round 10: Ch 1, [sc2tog] 3 times, join with slip st to first ch—3 sc remain.
Fasten off, leaving a 6" tail. Using G, embroider 2 rows of 3 dots as follows: Make an X, then embroider one more straight line across the X. Using yarn needle threaded with tail, stitch Body to Head.

FINISHING

Hanging Chains (make 8)
Using A, chain 100, leaving a 6" tail at both ends.
Tie 1 chain in a bow around base of each upright stem on Hoop (4 chains used); put a dab of glue behind each half of the bow to secure it. Tie the 4 remaining chains to the hoop, half way between each upright stem.

Happy Flowers: The Flowers are suspended on the Chains that are between the upright stems; thread one yarn end into a darning needle, take it through the top petal of the flower, a couple of rows from the edge of the petal; tie a small bow, then tie the loops in a knot. Trim the ends; place a dab of glue on the knots to secure them.

Baby Bugs: The Bugs are suspended from the Chains at the upright stems. Find the balance point on each Bug by inserting a darning needle into the Bug; hold up the darning needle to see if the Bug hangs properly from this point. Thread the yarn end from one of the hanging chains into a darning needle, and take it through the balance point on the Bug; tie a small bow, then tie the loops in a knot. Trim the ends; place a dab of glue on the knots to secure them.

8

BABY BLANKET QUILT #8

Easy

designed by Marilyn Losse
Shown on page 23

FINISHED MEASUREMENTS

Blanket measures approximately 34"/86 cm wide x 45"/114 cm long

MATERIALS

Medium/Worsted Weight Yarn (4 MEDIUM)
Shown in:
Caron International's Simply Soft Brites (100% acrylic; 6 oz/170 g, approx 315 yds/288 m):
#9610 Grape (A), 2 skeins
#9607 Limelight (B), 1 skein
#9608 Blue Mint (C), 1 skein
#9605 Mango (D), 1 skein
#9609 Berry Blue (E), 1 skein
#9604 Watermelon (F), 1 skein

Crochet Hook, size US G/6 (4 mm), or size to obtain gauge
Tapestry needle

GAUGE: Not critical for this project; each Basic Square measures approximately 2"/5 cm

STITCHES USED

Chain (ch) Double crochet (dc)
Single crochet (sc) Sl stitch (slip st)

BASIC SQUARE

Ch 4; join with a slip stitch to form a ring.
Round 1: Ch 3 (counts as dc), in the ring work 2 dc, ch 3 (corner), * 3 dc, ch 3 (corner); repeat from * twice, join with a slip stitch to beginning ch-3—4 sets of 3-dc, separated by ch-3 corner spaces.

NOTES

1. Each Block is comprised of 30 small Squares, 15 each (half-Blocks) of 2 different colors.
2. Two half-Blocks are then sewn together to complete one Block, resembling a Quilt Block.

BLANKET

Basic Squares

Work 180 in the following colors and quantities:
30 – B; 45 – C; 45 – D; 30 – E and 30 – F.

Assemble Blocks

Using tapestry needle and yarn, sew 15 same-color Squares into half-Blocks, then half-Blocks into **Blocks in the following Colorways** (see Diagram): **Block 1:** B/D; **Block 2:** F/E; **Block 3:** D/E; **Block 4:** B/C; **Block 5:** F/C; **Block 6:** C/D

Block Border (work on each Block)
Using A, join yarn with a slip stitch to any ch-3 (corner) space.
Round 1: **Ch 3, sc in same space as joining to form a loop (corner), *ch 3, sc in next ch-3 space; repeat from * to next corner; repeat from ** 3 times, end ch 3, join with a sl st to base of first corner loop.
Round 2: Sl st in first corner, ch 3 (counts as dc), work [2 dc, ch 3 (corner), 3 dc] in same corner, *work 3 dc in each ch-3 space of Rnd 1 to corner (do not ch 1 between 3-dc clusters), work [3 dc, ch 3 (corner), 3 dc] in corner; repeat from

* twice, work 3 dc in each ch-3 space across to beginning ch-3, join with a sl st to beginning ch-3.

Round 3: Slip stitch in first corner, ch 3 (counts as dc), work [2 dc, ch 3, 3 dc] in same corner, * work 3 dc between each 3-dc cluster of Round 2 to corner, work [3 dc, ch 3, 3 dc] in corner; repeat from * twice, work 3 dc between each 3-dc cluster across to beginning ch-3, join with a slip stitch to beginning ch-3.

Fasten off.

Assemble 6 Blocks to form center of Blanket (see Diagram).

Blanket Border

Using D, join yarn with a slip stitch to any corner.

Round 1: Work as for Round 1 of Block edging, working sc between 3-dc clusters instead of in ch-3 spaces.

Round 2: Slip stitch in first corner, ch 3 (counts as dc), work [2 dc, ch 3 (corner), 3 dc] in same corner, ch 1, * work [3 dc, ch 1] in each ch-3 space of Round 1 to corner, work [3 dc, ch 3 (corner), 3 dc] in corner; repeat from * twice, work [3 dc, ch 1] in each ch-3 space across to beginning ch-3, join with a slip stitch to beginning ch-3.

Fasten off D; join E with a slip stitch to any corner.

Round 3: Using E, ch 3 (counts as dc), work [2 dc, ch 3 (corner), 3 dc] in same corner, ch 1, * work [3 dc, ch 1] in each ch-1 space of Round 2 to corner, work [3 dc, ch 3 (corner), 3 dc] in corner; repeat from * twice, work [3 dc, ch 1] in each ch-1 space across to beginning ch-3, join with a slip stitch to beginning ch-3.

Fasten off E; join B with a slip stitch to any corner.

Rounds 4, 5 and 6: Using B, (F and C), work as for Round 3, fastening off and joining colors as indicated.

Rounds 7 and 8: Using A, work as for Round 3.

Shell Stitch Edging

Round 9: Continuing with A, ch 1, * sc in next st, skip 2 sts, work 5 dc in next st (Shell), skip 2 sts; repeat from * around, join with a slip stitch to first st.

Round 10: Work as Round 9, working a Shell in each sc and a sc in center st of each Shell around.

Fasten off.

Using tapestry needle, weave in all ends.

ASSEMBLY DIAGRAM

Not Shown to scale

KEY

- Grape (A)
- Limelight (B)
- Blue Mint (C)
- Mango (D)
- Berry Blue (E)
- Watermelon (F)

QUILT BLOCK

KEY

- Color 1
- Color 2

Baby's Flowers Blanket #9

Intermediate

designed by Martha Brooks Stein
Shown on back cover

FINISHED MEASUREMENTS:
Approximately 37"/94cm x 48"/122cm

MATERIALS
Medium/Worsted Weight Yarn (4 MEDIUM)
Shown in:
Caron International's Simply Soft Brites (100% acrylic; 6 oz/170 g, 315 yds/288 m skein):
#9606 Lemonade (A), 4 skeins
#9605 Mango (B), 2 skeins
#9604 Watermelon (C), 2 skeins
#9610 Grape (D), 2 skeins
#9609 Berry Blue (E), 2 skeins
#9607 Limelight (F), 2 skeins

Crochet Hook, size US I/9 (5.5mm), or size to obtain gauge
Tapestry needle

GAUGE: Each Square = 3 1/4" x 3 1/4"/8.3cm x 8.3cm

STITCHES USED
Chain (ch) Double crochet (dc)
Half double crochet (hdc)
Single crochet (sc) Slip stitch (sl st)

SQUARES (make 154)
Using first color (see Assembly Diagram Key for Colorways), chain 3, join with a slip st to form a ring.
Round 1 – Star (center): Ch 4 (counts as first dc, ch 2), in the ring, work [dc, ch 2] 7 times, join with slip st in second ch of beginning ch-4—8 dc, 8 ch-2 spaces. Fasten off first color.
Round 2: Join second color with a slip st in any ch-2 space; ch 2 (counts as dc), dc in same space, * work 3 hdc in next ch-2 space, [2 dc, ch 2, 2 dc] in next ch-2 space (corner); repeat from * twice, end 3 hdc in next ch-2 space, 2 dc in beginning ch-2 space, join with hdc (counts as corner ch-2) in top of beginning ch-2—3 hdc each side; 4 corners.
Round 3 – Joining Round (see Joining instructions): Ch 2 (counts as dc), dc in same corner space, * ch 1, work 2 dc in space between second dc and first hdc, ch 1, work 2 dc in space between third hdc and first dc, ch 1, work [2 dc, ch 2, 2 dc] in corner space; repeat from * twice (3 sides worked), end ch 1, work 2 dc in space between dc and hdc, ch 1, work 2 dc in space between hdc and dc, ch 1, work 2 dc in beginning corner space, ch 2, join with slip st in top of beginning ch-2—2 (dc-2), 3 ch-1 spaces on each side edge; 4 corners). Fasten off; weave in all ends.

NOTES
1. Make all Star centers first; weave in ends.
2. On Beginning Square, work Rounds 2 and 3.
3. On remaining Squares, work Round 2, then work Round 3, joining as-you-go using either One-Side Join, or Two-Side Join instructions. Note: Joining Diagram shows 4 squares as an example

of these 2 types of joining; X and Z will always be Squares that have been joined, W (working Square) will be the one being joined as-you-go.

STAR CENTERS (make 25 each using F and A (Colorways 1 and 6); make 26 each using E, D, C and B (Colorways 2, 3, 4 and 5).
Work Round 1 of Squares.

FIRST ROW of AFGHAN SQUARES
(See Assembly Diagram)
Beginning Square (make 1)
Work Rounds 1 – 3, using Colorway 6.

Second Square
Work Rounds 1 and 2, using Colorway 5.
Round 3: Work from * (the repeat) twice, end second repeat [2 dc, ch 1] in corner space —2 sides completed.

ONE-SIDE JOIN
(see Diagram – Z and W)
Note: For the initial join at upper left-hand corner, W = Second Square (above) and Z = Beginning Square.
Holding wrong sides of W-square and Z-square together, sc in Z-square corner-space, work 2 dc in W-square corner, sc in next ch-1 space of Z-square, work 2 dc in space between second dc and first hdc of W-square, sc in ch-1 space of Z-square, work 2 dc in space between third hdc and first dc of W-square, sc in ch-1 space of Z-square, work 2 dc in corner space of W-square, sc in corner space of Z-square, ch 1, work 2 dc in corner space of W-square (One-Side Join completed); continue Round 3, ending with 2 dc in corner space at the beginning of the round, ch 2, join with slip st in top of beginning ch-2.
Fasten off; weave in all ends.

Continue in this manner, following Assembly Diagram for Colorways, until 11 Squares have been joined (top row of Diagram).

SECOND ROW of AFGHAN
First Square (left-hand side of Diagram)
Work as for Second Square above, joining to lower edge of Beginning Square using One-Side Join.

Next Working Square
Work Rounds 1 and 2, using Colorway 4.
Round 3: Work from * (the repeat) once, end [2 dc, ch 1] in corner space —1 side completed.

TWO-SIDE JOIN
(see Diagram – X, Z and W)
This is worked in the same manner as One-Side Join, working first with W and X held together, then with W and Z held together. In other words:

Holding wrong sides of W-square and X-square together, sc in corner space of X-square, work 2 dc in corner space of W-square, sc in next ch-1 space of X-square, work 2 dc in space between second dc and first hdc of W-square, sc in ch-1 space of X-square, work 2 dc in space between third hdc and first dc of W-square, sc in ch-1 space of X-square, work 2 dc in corner space of W-square, sc in corner space of X-square, ch 1 (one side joined).
Reposition squares, holding wrong sides

of Z-square and W-square together; sc in corner space of Z-square, work 2 dc in corner space of W-square, sc in ch-space of Z-square, work 2 dc in space between second dc and first hdc of W-square, sc in ch-1 space of Z-square, work 2 dc in space between third hdc and first dc of W-square, sc in ch-1 space of Z-square, work 2 dc in corner space of W-square, sc in corner space of Z-square, ch 1 (Two-Side Join completed); continue Round 3, ending with 2 dc in corner space at the beginning of the round, ch 2, join with slip st in top of beginning ch-2.
Fasten off.

Continue working from Assembly Diagram, following Colorways, until 14 rows of Squares have been completed and joined.

BORDER

Note: Work in top 2 loops of each st or in ch-space as indicated.

Round 1: Using A, slip st in any corner-space, ch 1, sc in same space, * sc in next 2 dc, [skip ch-space, sc in next 2 dc] 3 times, sc in corner-space of Square, sc in joining st, sc in corner-space of next Square; repeat from * across to next corner of Afghan, [sc, ch 2, sc] in corner; repeat from * around Afghan, working [sc, ch 2 sc] in next 2 corners of Afghan, end sc in beginning corner-space, join with hdc in beginning sc.

Round 2: Ch 1, sc in corner-space, ch 1, * [skip next sc, sc in next sc, ch 1] across to next corner of Afghan, [sc, ch 2, sc] in corner, ch 1; repeat from * around Afghan, end sc in beginning corner-space, join with hdc in beginning sc.

Round 3: Ch 4 (counts as dc, ch 2), dc in corner-space, * [(dc, ch 2, dc) in next ch-1 space] across to next corner of Afghan, [(dc, ch 2) twice, dc] in corner; repeat from * around Afghan, end dc in beginning corner-space, join with hdc in second ch of beginning ch-4.

Round 4: Ch 5 (counts as dc, ch 3), dc in joining corner-space, [(dc, ch 3) twice, dc] in next ch-2 corner-space, * [dc, ch 3, dc] in each ch-2 space across to next corner, [(dc, ch 3) twice, dc] in both ch-2 corner-spaces; repeat from * around Afghan, end dc in beginning corner-space, join with dc in second ch of beginning ch-5.

Round 5: Ch 5 (counts as dc, ch 3), dc in joining corner-space, [(dc, ch 3) twice, dc] in each of next 3 ch-3 corner-spaces, * [dc, ch 3, dc] in each ch-3 space across to next corner of Afghan, [(dc, ch 3 twice, dc] in corner-space; repeat from* around Afghan, end dc in first ch-3 corner space, ch 3, join with slip st in second ch of beginning ch-5.
Fasten off.

FINISHING

Using tapestry needle, weave in all ends.

ASSEMBLY DIAGRAM

6	5	4	3	2	1	6	5	4	3	2
5	4	3	2	1	6	5	4	3	2	1
4	3	2	1	6	5	4	3	2	1	6
3	2	1	6	5	4	3	2	1	6	5
2	1	6	5	4	3	2	1	6	5	4
1	6	5	4	3	2	1	6	5	4	3
6	5	4	3	2	1	6	5	4	3	2
5	4	3	2	1	6	5	4	3	2	1
4	3	2	1	6	5	4	3	2	1	6
3	2	1	6	5	4	3	2	1	6	5
2	1	6	5	4	3	2	1	6	5	4
1	6	5	4	3	2	1	6	5	4	3
6	5	4	3	2	1	6	5	4	3	2
5	4	3	2	1	6	5	4	3	2	1

KEY

Colorways:
Round 1 / Rounds 2 and 3 - total number.

Diagram shows color for Rounds 2 and 3

- 1 Colorway 1: F / C - 25
- 2 Colorway 2: E / B - 26
- 3 Colorway 3: D / A - 26
- 4 Colorway 4: C / F - 26
- 5 Colorway 5: B / E - 26
- 6 Colorway 6: A / D - 25

Joining Diagram

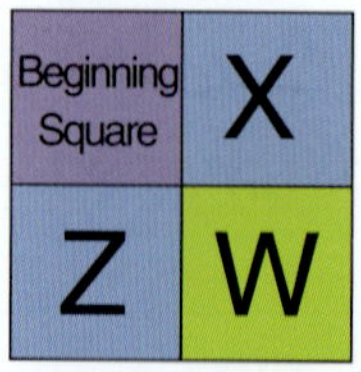

W: Working Square
X: Square above Working Square.
Z: Square beside Working Square

For One-Side Join, designate Square to the left of W as Z.

For Two-Side Join, designate Square above W as X; Square to the left as Z.

GENERAL INSTRUCTIONS

ABBREVIATIONS

CC	Contrasting Color
ch	chain
cm	centimeters
dc	double crochet
hdc	half double crochet
inc	increase
MC	Main Color
mm	millimeters
rem	remaining
rep	repeat
sc	single crochet
ssc	shallow single crochet
st(s)	stitches
tog	together
tr	treble crochet
yo	yarn over

* — work instructions following * as many **more** times as indicated in addition to the first time.

\+ — work all instructions from first to second **as many** times as specified.

( ) or [ ] — work enclosed instruction as many times as specified by the number immediately following **or** work all enclosed instructions in the stitch or space indicated **or** contains explanatory remarks.

colon (:) — the number(s) given after a colon at the end of a row or round denote(s) the number of stitches or spaces you should have on that row or round.

GAUGE

Exact GAUGE is **essential** for proper size. Before beginning your project, make the sample swatch given in the individual instructions in the yarn or thread and hook specified. After completing the swatch, measure it, counting your stitches and rows or rounds carefully. If your swatch is larger or smaller than specified, **make another, changing hook size to get the correct gauge.** Keep trying until you find the size hook that will give you the specified gauge.